यह मेरी किताब है!
(yah   meree   kitaab   hai!)

Gnaana Publishing
PO Box 10513
Fullerton, CA 92838
inspire@gnaana.com
www.gnaana.com

Text © 2015 Aruna Hatti
Illustrations © 2015 Kalyani Ganapathy
Book design by Sara Petrous

10 9 8 7 6 5 4 3 2

Cataloging-in-Publication Data available at the Library of Congress.

ISBN 978-1-943018-22-2 (Book)
ISBN 978-1-943018-23-9 (Book with Audio CD)

a *is for* anaar
My First
Hindi Alphabet Book

Written by
Aruna Hatti

Illustrations by
Kalyani Ganapathy

gnaana

नमस्ते!
(namaste!)

मेरा नाम विद्या है.
(mera naam vidya hai.)

I'm from India, and I speak हिन्दी.
(hindi)

Come and learn the हिन्दी वर्णमाला with me!
(hindi   varNamaala)

Hindi is spoken by almost 500 million people worldwide. It is the 4th most widely spoken language in the world! Hindi is one of the official languages of India and of Fiji. Hindi is written in the Devanagari script – an ancient writing system with roots dating back to the 4th century BCE!

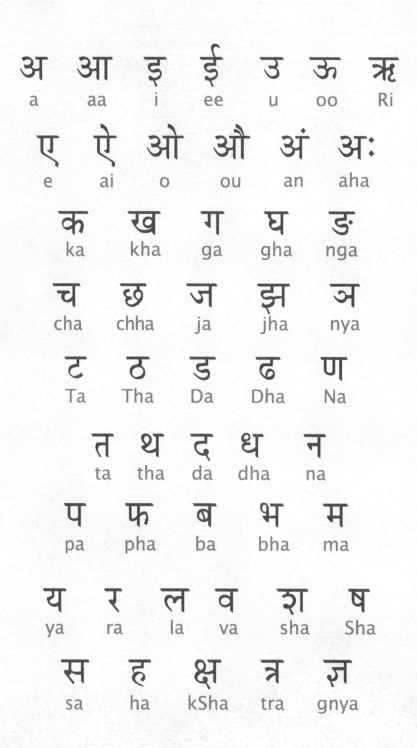

अ	आ	इ	ई	उ	ऊ	ऋ
a	aa	i	ee	u	oo	Ri

ए	ऐ	ओ	औ	अं	अः
e	ai	o	ou	an	aha

क	ख	ग	घ	ङ
ka	kha	ga	gha	nga

च	छ	ज	झ	ञ
cha	chha	ja	jha	nya

ट	ठ	ड	ढ	ण
Ta	Tha	Da	Dha	Na

त	थ	द	ध	न
ta	tha	da	dha	na

प	फ	ब	भ	म
pa	pha	ba	bha	ma

य	र	ल	व	श	ष
ya	ra	la	va	sha	Sha

स	ह	क्ष	त्र	ज्ञ
sa	ha	kSha	tra	gnya

अ
(a)

आ
(aa)

इ
(i)

ई
(ee)

In हिन्दी, the vowels (called स्वर),
(hindi)   (svar)

come first.

ए
(ai)

ए
(e)

ऋ
(Ri)

ऊ
(oo)

उ
(u)

There are 13 vowels.

ओ
(o)

औ
(ou)

अं
(an)

अः
(aha)

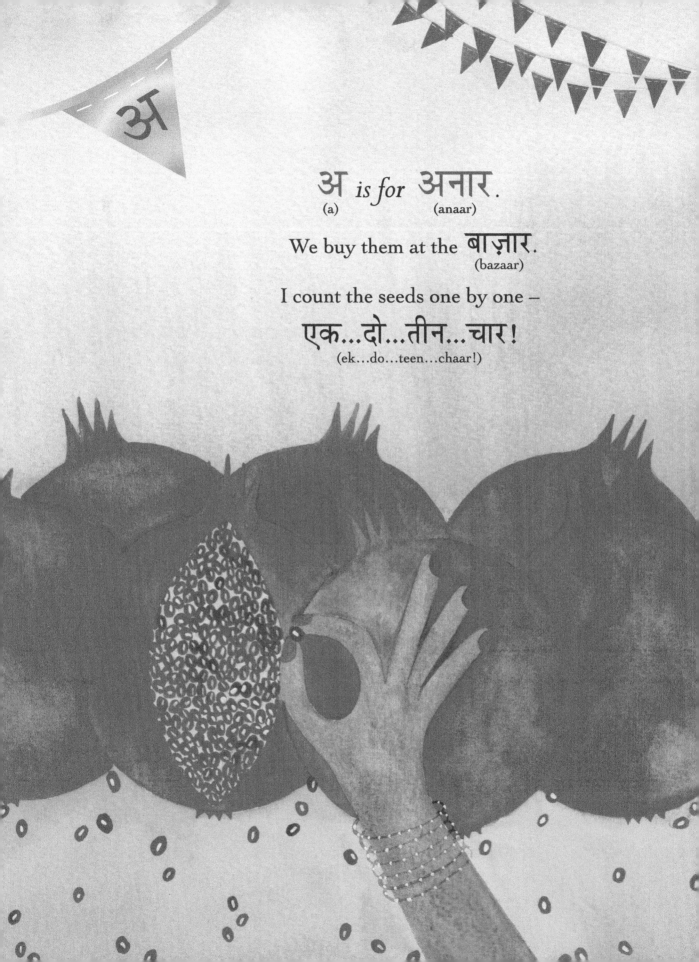

अ *is for* अनार.
(a)   (anaar)

We buy them at the बाज़ार.
                        (bazaar)

I count the seeds one by one –

एक...दो...तीन...चार!
(ek...do...teen...chaar!)

आ *is for* आंखें.
(aa)　　　(aankhen)

They wink and blink and spy.
Curious sights every day –

यह क्या है?
(yah kyaa hai?)

इ *is for* इंद्रधनुष,
(i) (indr'dhanuSh)
stretching in the sky.
Or in the sweet shop –
yummy मिठाई!
(miThai!)

ई *is for* ईंटें,
(ee)   (eenTen)

stacked in my room.
I build super castles —
मैं रानी हूँ!
(main raanee hoon!)

उ *is for* उल्लू
(u)　　　　　(ulloo)

(oo... oo... oo...)

He keeps us all awake at night,

including our pet ऊँट.
(oonT)

ऋ *is for* ऋषि,
(Ri)   (RiShi)

deep in Vedic concentration,
अगस्त्य is a famous one.
(agastya)

He once drank up
an entire ocean!

ए *is for* एक,
(e) (ek)

very special indeed.

नानी's ऐनक on the chair:
(naanee) (ainak)

"That was my only pair!"

ओ *is for* ओखली.
(o)   (okhlee)

दादी grinds the धनिया,
(daadee)   (dhaniya)

while she tells me tales of

औरंगज़ेब,
(aurangzeb)

who ruled over
parts of India!

अं *is for* अंगूर –
(an)　　　　　　　(angoor)

काला, लाल, या हरा.
(kaala,　　laal,　　yaa　hara)

Which brings us to the final vowel.

How does it go? अः!
(aha!)

Hindi has 36 consonants (called व्यंजन).
(vyanjan)

Let's start with the first 5:

क
(ka)

ख
(kha)

ग
(ga)

घ
(gha)

ङ
(nga)

क *is for* कहानी,
(ka)   (kahaanee)

like

खरगोश और कछुआ.
(khargosh   aur   kachh'ua)

In the story, they had a race —

Do you know: क्या हुआ?
(kyaa hu'aa?)

ग *is for* गाजर.
(ga)   (gaajar)

My घोड़ा likes them tall.
(ghorda)

चलो! Let's go –
(chalo!)

before you eat them all!

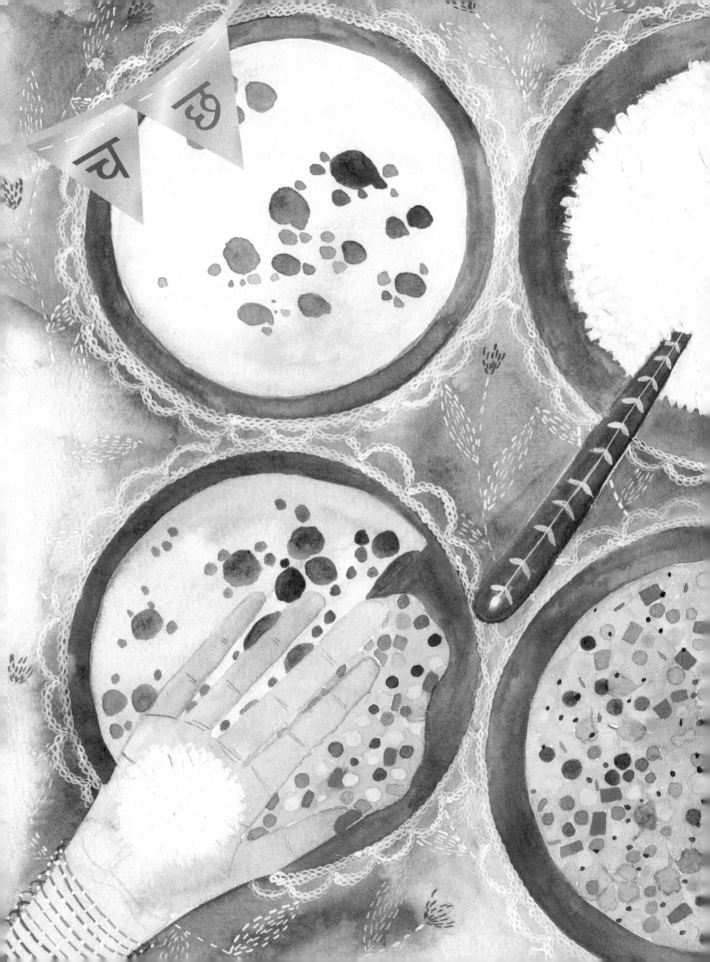

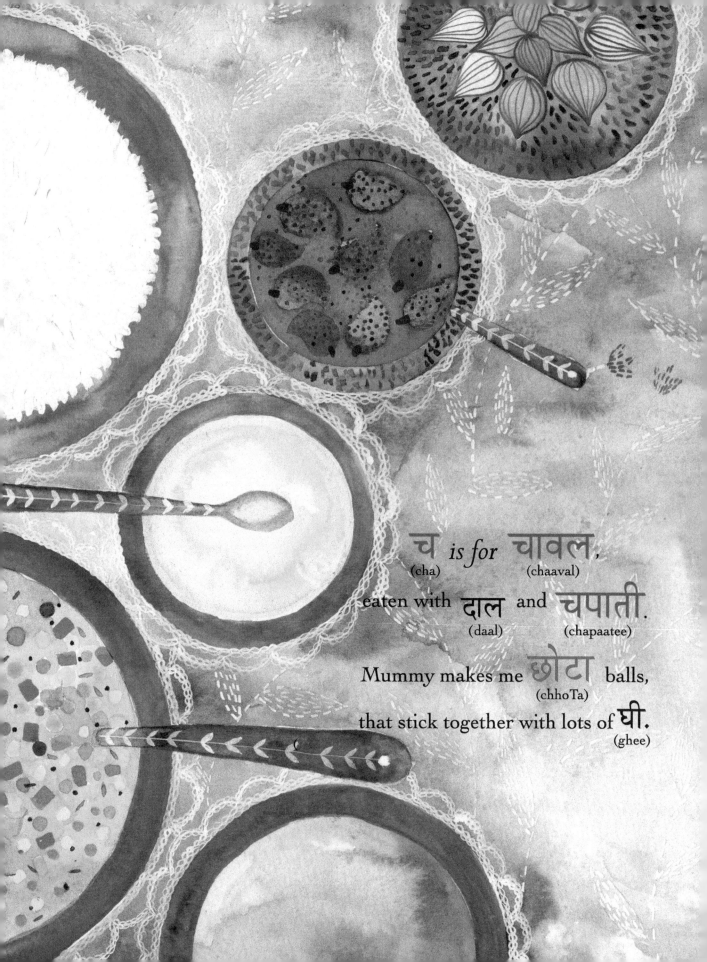

च *is for* चावल,
(cha) (chaaval)

eaten with दाल and चपाती.
(daal) (chapaatee)

Mummy makes me छोटा balls,
(chhoTa)

that stick together with lots of घी.
(ghee)

ज *is for* जूते –
(ja)   (joote)

shiny, jeweled, glamorous.

Ruby chewed the green ones once,

and मौसी, she screamed बस!
(mausee)   (bas!)

झ *is for* झूला,
(jha)   (jhoola)

hanging from our mango tree.
Monkeys being sly and silly –

मस्ती! मस्ती!
(mastee!) (mastee!)

ट *is for* टिफ़िन –
(Ta)　　　　(Tiphin)

रोटी, सब्ज़ी, a boiled अंडा.
(roTee, sabzee,)　　　　　(anDa)

नींबू पानी for my drink –
(neemboo paanee)

ठंडा! ठंडा!
(ThanDa! ThanDa!)

ड *is for* डांडिया.
(Da)   (DanDiya)

नवरात्री – we're out of control!
(navraatree)

दीदी dances गरबा रास,
(deedee)   (garba   raas)

and I bang on my ढोल!
                        (Dhol!)

त
(ta)

थ
(tha)

द
(da)

ध
(dha)

न
(na)

त *is for* तबला.
(ta)   (tabla)

I'll be famous someday, I know.
I even play beats on my

थाली.
(thaalee)

"विद्या...खाना खाओ!"
("Vidya....khaana khaa'o!")

is for

(da)   (deeya)

We light them before our God.

And when I say prayers on

(divaalee)

I say धन्यवाद.

(dhanyavaad)

न *is for* नाक.
(na)   (naak)

I smell spices all around me.

My favorite is the इलायची.
                      (ilaay'chee)

for बिरयानी and चाय tea.
   (biryaanee)   (chaay)

प *is for* पेड़ –
(pa) (per)

orange, guava, and fig.
It doesn't seem quite logical:
How does the
फूल turn into फल?
(phool) (phal)

ब is for बारिश.
(ba) (baarish)

The monsoon – what a show!

Oh no, the door is open!

दरवाज़ा बंद करो!
(darvaaza band karo!)

भ *is for* भारत,
(bha)   (bhaarat)

another name for home.
I name the states with panache –
दादा claps and says, शाबाश!
(daada)   (shaabaash!)

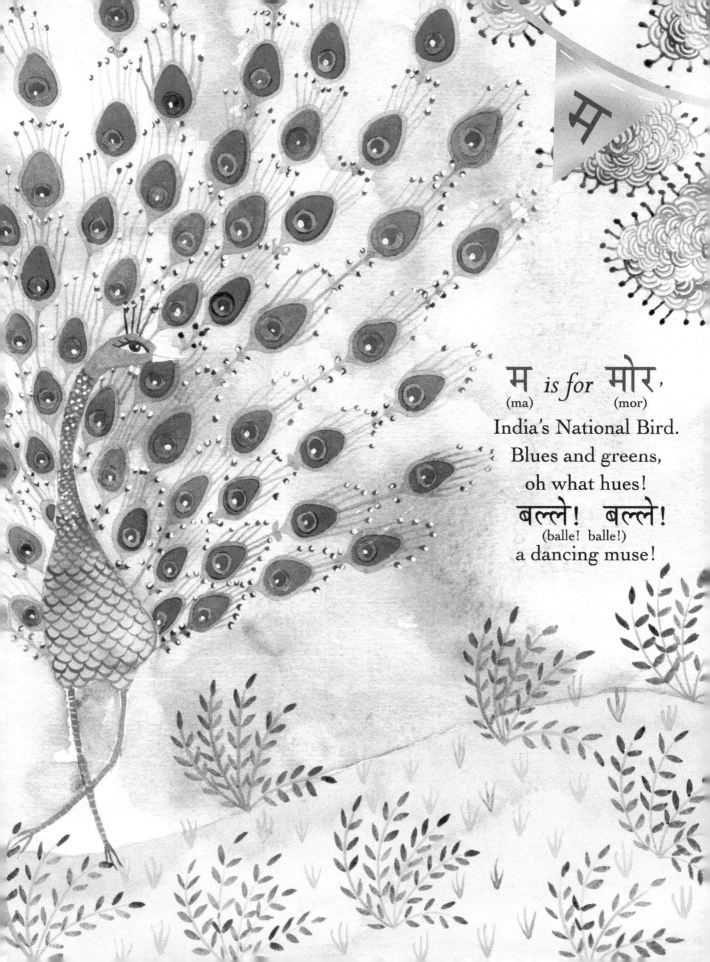

म *is for* मोर,
(ma)　　　(mor)
India's National Bird.
Blues and greens,
oh what hues!
बल्ले! बल्ले!
(balle! balle!)
a dancing muse!

य *is for* यमुना,
(ya)   (yamuna)

a river passing नई दिल्ली.
(new   dillee)

Temples, mosques and हवेली –
(havelee)

and courtyards

filled with रंगोली.
(rangolee)

ल *is for* लंका –
(la)   (lanka)

रावण's lair.
(raavaN's)

" राम will come for me through your gate."
(raam)

"He is विष्णु. He'll seal your fate!"
(viShNu)

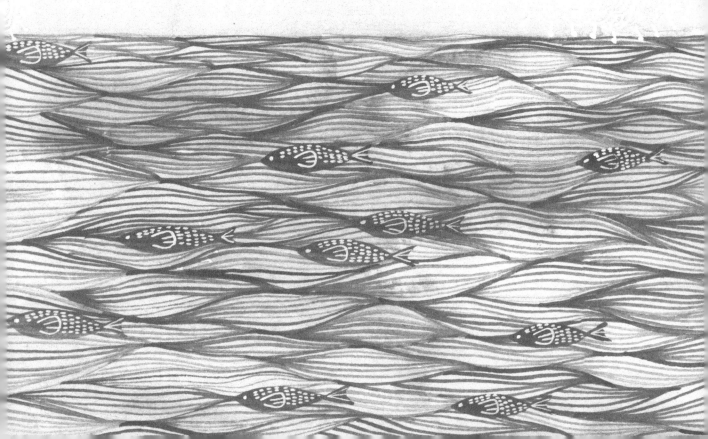

श *is for* शंख,
(sha)　　　(shankh)

that wash upon the shore.

She sells sea shells

shaped like षट्कोण!
(ShaTkoN)

स *is for* साँप,
(sa)   (saamp)

lurking in the trees.

Oh, no! It's coming after me —

जल्दी!   जल्दी!
(jaldee!)   (jaldee!)

is for ,
(ha) (haathee)

parading in my dreams.

, , , that's all from me —
(kSha, tra, gna)

शुभ रात्रि!
(shubh raatri!)

Glossary

In order of appearance:

नमस्ते	/na-ma-ste/	A respectful Hindu greeting used for both "hello" and "good-bye," spoken while holding the palms together vertically.
मेरा नाम विद्या है.	/me-ra naam vi-dya hai/	My name is Vidya.
हिन्दी वर्णमाला	/hin-di va-rNa-maa-la/	Hindi alphabets.
अनार	/a-naa-r/	A pomegranate.
बाज़ार	/ba-zaa-r/	A marketplace or shopping area, typically filled with stalls and street vendors.
एक...दो...तीन...चार!	/e-k, do, tee-n, chaa-r/	Counting: 1, 2, 3, 4.
आंखें	/aan-khen/	Eyes; plural form of आंख (/aan-kh/ - eye).
यह क्या है?	/yah kyaa hai/	What is this?
इंद्रधनुष	/in-dr-dha-nu-Sh/	A rainbow (literally, "Lord Indra's bow").
मिठाई	/mi-Tha-i/	Indian sweets.
ईंटें	/een-Ten/	Bricks; plural form of ईंट (/een-T/ - brick).
मैं रानी हूँ!	/main raa-nee hoon/	I am queen!
उल्लू	/u-lloo/	An owl.
ऊँट	/oon-T/	A camel.
ऋषि	/Ri-Shi/	A holy Hindu sage.
अगस्त्य	/a-ga-stya/	One of the saptarishis (seven sages) described in the Vedas and Hindu literature. The story of Rishi Agastya drinking up the ocean is mentioned in The Puranas.
एक	/e-k/	The number one.
नानी	/naa-nee/	Grandmother (maternal).
ऐनक	/ai-na-k/	Eyeglasses.
ओखली	/o-kh-lee/	A small mortar, typically used for grinding spices.
दादी	/daa-dee/	Grandmother (paternal).
धनिया	/dha-ni-ya/	Coriander, the seeds of which are used as a spice.
औरंगज़ेब	/au-ran-g-ze-b/	Sixth Mughal Emperor who ruled over many parts of the Indian subcontinent from 1658-1707.
अंगूर	/an-goo-r/	Grapes.
काला, लाल, या हरा	/kaa-la, laa-l, yaa ha-ra/	Black, red, and green
कहानी	/ka-haa-nee/	A tale, story.
खरगोश और कछुआ	/kha-r-go-sh au-r ka-chhu-aa/	The Hare and the Tortoise
क्या हुआ ?	/kyaa hu-aa/	What happened?
गाजर	/gaa-ja-r/	A carrot.

घोड़ा	/gho-rda/	A horse.
चलो !	/cha-lo/	Let's go!
चावल	/chaa-va-l/	Rice.
दाल	/daa-l/	Lentils, typically boiled and spiced for eating.
चपाती	/cha-paa-tee/	A thin circle of unleavened wheat bread.
छोटा	/chho-Ta/	Small.
घी	/ghee/	Clarified butter.
जूते	/joo-te/	A pair of shoes.
मौसी	/mau-see/	Aunt (maternal).
बस !	/ba-s/	Enough! Stop!
झूला	/jhoo-la/	A swing.
मस्ती ! मस्ती !	/ma-stee ma-stee/	Fun! Fun!
टिफिन	/Ti-phi-n/	A light mid-day meal; can also mean "lunch."
रोटी	/ro-Tee/	A circle of unleavened wheat bread, which can be thin or thick.
सब्ज़ी	/sa-bzee/	A vegetable curry.
अंडा	/an-Da/	An egg.
नींबू पानी	/neem-boo paa-nee/	Lemonade (literally "lemon water").
ठंडा! ठंडा!	/Than-Da Than-Da/	Cold! Cold! (Refreshing and cooling.)
डांडिया	/Daan-Di-ya/	A pair of sticks used when performing Dandiya Raas, a traditional folk dance from Gujarat popular during the Navratri festival. The dandiyas of the dance are symbolic of the swords/weapons used during Goddess Durga's battle with Mahishasura.
नवरात्री	/na-v-raa-tree/	A Hindu festival celebrated over nine nights and ten days during September/October honoring womanhood and Goddess Durga.
दीदी	/dee-dee/	Elder sister.
गरबा रास	/gar-ba raa-s/	A devotional Gujarati dance performed in concentric circles during the Navratri festival in honor of Goddess Durga.
ढोल	/Dho-l/	A large elongated, double-headed drum.
तबला	/ta-b-la/	A pair of small hand drums fundamental to Hindustani classical music. Individually, the larger daya is played with the right hand and the baya is played with the left hand.
थाली	/thaa-lee/	A flat plate, usually metal.
विद्या...खाना खाओ!	/vi-dya khaa-na khaa-o/	"Vidya, eat your food!"
दीया	/dee-ya/	A small oil lamp, typically made with clay, used in prayer and worship. During the festival of Diwali (Deepavali), houses are decorated with rows of diyas.

दिवाली	/ði-vaa-lee/	Also called Deepavali, it is one of India's major holidays celebrated by Hindus, Sikhs, Jains, and Buddhists. Diwali generally falls in the months of October or November.
धन्यवाद	/ðha-nya-vaa-ð/	Thank you.
नाक	/naa-k/	The nose.
इलायची	/i-laa-y-chee/	Cardamom – a highly-aromatic spice used to flavor Indian foods, sweets, and drinks.
बिरयानी	/bi-r-yaa-nee/	A rice dish from India made with highly-seasoned rice and vegetables, and sometimes meat or fish.
चाय	/cha-y/	A type of Indian tea made by boiling the tea leaves with milk, sugar, cardamom, and other spices. Note, the use of "cha-y tea" in the book is redundant, but was used for rhyming purposes.
पेड़	/pe-r/	A tree.
फूल	/phoo-l/	A flower.
फल	/pha-l/	Fruit.
बारिश	/baa-ri-sh/	Rain.
दरवाज़ा बंद करो!	/ða-r-vaa-za ban-ð ka-ro/	Close the door!
भारत	/bhaa-ra-t/	The Republic of India translates to Bhaarat Ganaraajya in Hindi.
दादा	/ðaa-ða/	Grandfather (paternal).
शाबाश!	/shaa-baa-sh/	Applause; praise. A term used to signal commendation for an achievement.
मोर	/mo-r/	A peacock.
बल्ले! बल्ले!	/ba-lle ba-lle/	A phrase, of Punjabi origin, which connotes a feeling of joy and happiness, often accompanied by dancing.
यमुना	/ya-mu-na/	A river in northern India (7th longest in the nation) which passes by Delhi and Agra.
नई दिल्ली	/na-i ði-llee/	New Delhi.
रंगोली	/ran-go-lee/	Painted decoration.
लंका	/lan-ka/	Sri Lanka.
रावण	/raa-va-N/	The principal villain in The Ramayana and ruler of Lanka, who was defeated and killed by Ram.
राम	/raa-m/	Lord Vishnu's seventh avatar and the protagonist of The Ramayana.
विष्णु	/vi-ShNu/	The Hindu god regarded as the preserver of the universe during each period of its existence, and who becomes manifest in the world in successive avatars.
शंख	/shan-kh/	A conch shell.
षट्कोण	/Sha-T-ko-N/	A hexagon.
साँप	/saam-p/	A snake.
जल्दी! जल्दी!	/ja-lðee ja-lðee/	Hurry! Hurry!
हाथी	/haa-thee/	An elephant.
शुभ रात्रि !	/shu-bh raa-tri/	Good night!

चलो हिन्दी बोले!
(chalo hindi bole!)

Let's talk in Hindi!

नमस्ते! मेरा नाम विद्या है. तुम्हारा नाम क्या है?
(Namaste! Mera naam Vidya hai. Tumhaara naam kyaa hai?)

Namaste! My name is Vidya. What's your name?

मेरा नाम _____ है.
(Mera naam _____ hai.)

My name is _____.

मैं दस साल की हूँ. तुम कितने साल की हो?
(Main das saal kee hoon. Tum kitne saal kee ho?)

I am ten years old. How old are you?

मैं _____ साल की हूँ.
(Main _____ saal kee hoon.)

I am ___ years old. (said by female)

मैं _____ साल का हूँ.
(Main _____ saal kaa hoon.)

I am ___ years old. (said by male)

तुम स्कूल जाते हो?
Tum skool jaate ho?

Do you go to school?

हाँ, मैं स्कूल जाती हूँ.
Ha, main skool jaatee hoon.

Yes, I go to school. (said by female)

हाँ, मैं स्कूल जाता हूँ.
Ha, main skool jaata hoon.

Yes, I go to school. (said by male)

तुम कौनसे कक्षा में पड़ते हो?
Tum kounse kakSha men parte ho?

What class (grade) do you study in?

मैं ___ कक्षा में पड़ती हूँ.
Main ___ kakSha men partee hoon.

I study in _____ class (grade). (said by female).

मैं ___ कक्षा में पड़ता हूँ.
Main ___ kakSha men parta hoon.

I study in _____ class (grade). (said by male).

Hindi Cardinals:			Hindi Ordinals (use feminine for "grade"):		
1	एक	/e-k/	1st	पहला/पहली	/pa-ha-la/, /pa-ha-lee/
2	दो	/do/	2nd	दूसरा/दूसरी	/doo-sa-ra/, /doo-sa-ree/
3	तीन	/tee-n/	3rd	तीसरा/तीसरी	/tee-sa-ra/, /tee-sa-ree/
4	चार	/chaa-r/	4th	चौथा/चौथी	/chou-tha/, /chou-thee/
5	पांच	/paan-ch/	5th	पांचवां/पांचवीं	/paan-ch-vaan/, /paan-ch-veen/
6	छह	/chha-h/	6th	छठा/छठी	/chha-Tha/, /chha-Thee/
7	सात	/saa-t/	7th	सातवां/सातवीं	/saa-t-vaan/, /saa-t-veen/
8	आठ	/aa-Th/	8th	आठवां/आठवीं	/aa-Th-vaan/, /aa-Th-veen/
9	नौ	/nou/	9th	नौवां/नौवीं	/nou-vaan/, /nou-veen/
10	दस	/da-s/	10th	दसवां/दसवीं	/da-s-vaan/, /da-s-veen/

मैं नई दिल्ली में रहती हूँ. तुम कहां रहते/ रहती हो?
Main new dillee men rahtee hoon. Tum kahan rahte / rahtee ho?

मैं ____ में रहती हूँ.
Main _____ men rahtee hoon.

मैं ____में रहता हूँ.
Main _____ men rahta hoon.

मेरी एक बहन है, वह मुझसे बड़ी है.
Meree ek bahan hai, voh mujhse baree hai.

और तुम? तुम्हारे कितने भाई – बहन हैं?
Aur tum? Tumhaare kitne bhaa-ee - bahan hain?

मेरा ____ भाई हैं.
Mera _____ baa-ee hain.

मेरी ____ बहन (बहनें) हैं.
Meree _____ bahan (bahanen) hain.

मेरे ____ भाई हैं.
Mere _____ baa-ee hain.

मेरी ____ बहन (बहनें) हैं.
Meree _____ bahan (bahanen) hain.

मेरा पसंदीदा रंग नीला है.
Meraa pasandeeda rang neela hai.

तुमको कौन सा रंग पसंद है?
Tumko koun saa rang pasand hai?

मेरा पसंदीदा रंग ____ है.
Meraa pasandeeda rang _____ hai.

फिर मिलेंगे! नमस्ते!
Phir milenge! Namaste!

I live in New Delhi. Where do you live?
* रहते *(rahte)* when asking male
* रहती *(rahtee)* when asking female

I live in ____. (said by female).

I live in ____. (said by male).

I have one sister, and she is older than me.

And you? Do you have any brothers or sisters?

(said by female):
I have ___ brother(s).

I have ___ sister(s).

(said by male):
I have ___ brother(s).

I have ___ sister(s).

My favorite color is blue.

What is your favorite color?

My favorite color is _____.

Goodbye!

Hindi Colors:					
Red	लाल	/laa-l/	Pink	गुलाबी	/gu-laa-bee/
Orange	नारंगी	/naa-ran-gee/	Black	काला	/kaa-laa/
Yellow	पीला	/pee-laa/	White	सफेद	/sa-phe-∂/
Green	हरा	/ha-raa/	Brown	भूरा	/bhoo-raa/
Blue	नीला	/nee-laa/	Gray	धूसर	/∂hoo-sa-r/
Purple	जामुनी	/jaa-mu-nee/			

CPSIA information can be obtained
at www.ICGtesting.com
Printed in the USA
BVOW05*2202290517
485445BV00011B/59/P